THE PRINCIPLES OF

Pretty Rooms

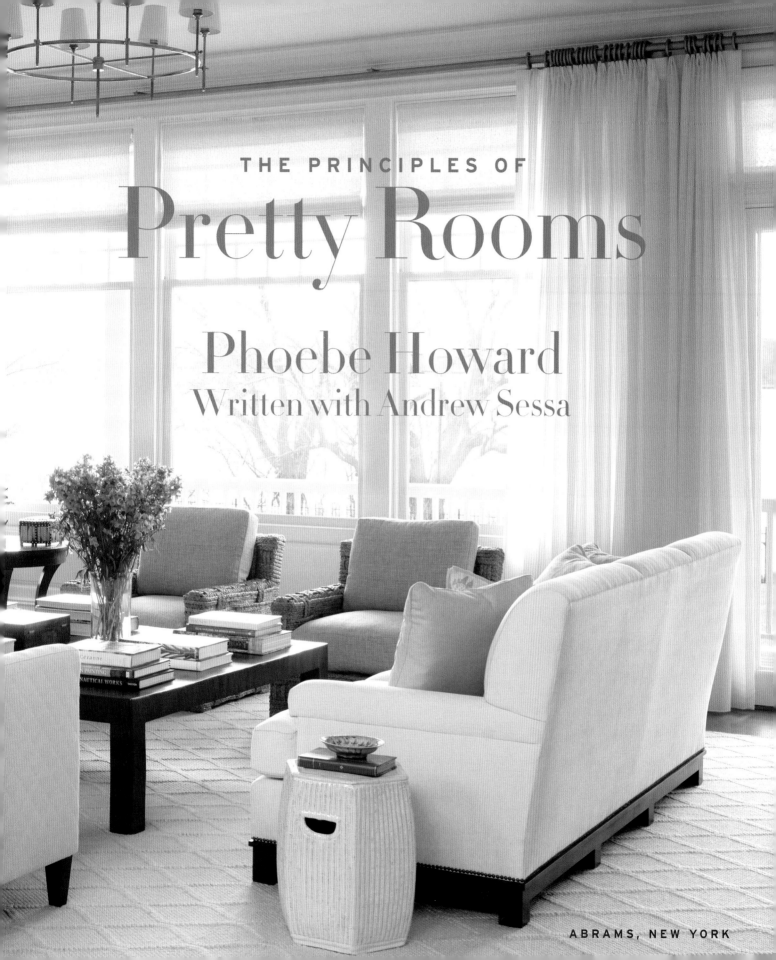

THE PRINCIPLES OF
Pretty Rooms

Phoebe Howard
Written with Andrew Sessa

ABRAMS, NEW YORK

CONTENTS

INTRODUCTION

i've been asked many times over the years to describe my style of decorating, and each and every time I circle back to one word: pretty. I decorate houses all over the country for all different kinds of people, but somewhere along the way, I realized that no matter where I am, I always apply the same principles—the Principles of Pretty Rooms—to create spaces that entice and enchant people, making them feel good, comfortable, and at home as soon as they enter.

Some rooms require you to think; they force you to constantly look around to notice different details that you may not have seen at first. These sorts of spaces are often architectural marvels, and their decoration follows suit. Pretty rooms, on the other hand, take the edge off, inviting you to relax and unwind. That's because pretty isn't complex or complicated. Rather, its simplicity and lack of fussiness help you design rooms that are warm, welcoming, and the furthest thing from intimidating. Any space that feels peaceful and tranquil—whether traditional or modern, neutral or colorful, nearby or far-flung—can be pretty.

Pretty pleases the eye and eases the mind. In that way, pretty itself is easy: easy to live with, and easy for you to achieve in your own home, too. Now more than ever, we want our spaces to be sanctuaries, safely allowing us to escape from the realities of everyday life and work. The Principles of Pretty Rooms allow you to create rooms that do just that.

My Southern roots cultivated my natural affinity for pretty. While I was growing up in northern Florida, I made frequent trips to my grandparents' farm in Alabama, and I managed to find pretty everywhere I looked. My four brothers

The Principles of Pretty Rooms help you create harmony among the architecture, furnishings, fabrics, rugs, lighting, and accessories in any room or residence. Each of these elements has its own important role to play, and each is of equal importance.

and I grew up in a nine-hundred-square-foot apartment above a garage, but I never thought of it as anything other than a big, beautiful house. It had high ceilings with exposed wooden rafters and walls clad in warm cedar. A round window set in each of its gabled ends flooded it with natural light. The fact that it sat right on the beach didn't hurt, either.

At her simple Alabama farmhouse, meanwhile, my grandmother cultivated a whole wall's worth of African violets, setting them on three shelves in front of a south-facing window. They weren't fancy or expensive, but they left a lasting impression. The warmth of the sun hitting them, the richness of the color of their flowers, and the velvety texture of their leaves made them seem like the most beautiful thing in the world. The same was true of the cut-glass decanters full of colored water that she placed in another window, and the handmade quilts, bedspreads, and crocheted blankets that added a sense of softness throughout her house.

We Southerners have a special talent for creating beautiful moments like these, and for making pretty seem effortless. But it actually takes careful planning and thoughtful execution to turn a space into an oasis of pretty. My goal for this book is to help you achieve the romance and tranquility of pretty in your own home. My Principles of Pretty Rooms (opposite) will serve as your primer, one that takes the guesswork out of making pretty possible.

And pretty very much *is* possible for anyone to achieve, anywhere. That's because it is exceptionally flexible. Unlike more prescribed aesthetics—minimalist modernism, for example—pretty knows no limits of style or era.

The three sections of this book take a look at pretty in practice in a variety of houses I designed in a trio of different settings—in the city, in the country, and at the beach. Each one benefits from a different set of elements specific to its setting and its owners' desires, but they all ultimately delight the senses because they adhere to the overarching principles that I apply to every interior.

I know you'll find these principles as useful as I do. Decorating with them makes pretty a piece of cake—and a beautifully decorated one, too.

THE PRINCIPLES
OF PRETTY ROOMS

These guidelines will help you make your project a beautiful success, no matter where your home is.

1. EMBRACE SYMMETRY Use pairs, whether perfectly matching or slightly mismatched, to achieve a sense of balance.

2. REDUCE COLOR CONTRASTS Temper the temperature of the hues you use. Pretty color is controlled color.

3. USE SOLIDS Patterns—including toiles, paisleys, stripes, ikats, and block prints—have their place, but they need to mix with solids.

4. MIX OLD AND NEW The patina of antiques adds the sort of romance, nostalgia, and timelessness that defines the best pretty rooms.

5. GO SOFT You'll want upholstered pieces, cushions, and pillows aplenty, as well as gently curving lines throughout.

6. LAYER IT UP This isn't just for beds, or for cool-weather locales. It applies to rugs, window treatments, and more.

7. INCORPORATE DRESSMAKER DETAILS Tailor the look of your room with elements such as embroidery, passameterie, ribbon, and hand stitching.

8. DECK THE WALLS Deciding what art and mirrors go where shouldn't be an afterthought. Think about wall hangings early.

9. FIND YOUR LIGHT Focus on creating softness and pools of light, something that feels warm and maximizes sunlight.

10. BE ORGANIZED The prettiest rooms come out of careful planning. I live and die by a floor plan.

city

When you're otherwise surrounded by the hustle and bustle of urban living, a pretty, personal home serves as a peaceful and welcoming oasis. In the city, you'll want to create a space that stands in contrast to its surroundings—one that mitigates the challenges found outside its walls. Pretty city homes are as protective as they are peaceful, and as sheltering as they are fabulous.

In urban environments, the prettiest interiors make shutting out sound among their first priorities. Doing so doesn't have to be a purely practical matter. Some of the easiest ways to ensure a space stays quiet also happen to be beautiful. Think about absorbing sound by layering seagrass and oriental carpets and by using several different window treatments. Upholstering walls with textiles adds noise-dampening qualities as well as texture, pattern, and tailored detailing. These elements let the city be seen, but not heard, from your home.

Space is almost always at a premium in urban settings. To prevent a room from feeling small, you'll need to be especially careful about how you curate everything that goes in it. Among the best ways to do this is to choose furnishings that can do double duty of one kind or another; then make sure that each piece adheres to at least one pretty principle, or even two or three. Sofas and beds with hidden storage are wonderful, and beautifully cushioned window seats are a great way to make a space serve dual purposes. Replace a traditional coffee table with an antique trunk that provides room for blankets or extra pillows, or an ottoman, which offers an opportunity to bring in softness and curves, as well as color and pattern. Furnishings and features such as these will help you live beautifully even if you don't live large.

Shimmering surfaces and materials also add beauty to petite rooms by expanding the sense of space and reflecting light. This means using mirrors

When a space offers a beautifully framed peek into an adjacent, equally lovely area—like the view from living area to foyer provided by the arched opening here—make sure the placement of your furniture leaves room for the view.

and metals, and not just in the expected places. Polished brass or chrome tables, mirrored backsplash tile or even cabinetry, and reflective light fixtures can bring on a general feeling of lightness and brightness. Iridescent paint finishes, high-gloss painted or tea paper ceilings, and metallic wallpaper also give spaces a luminous glow.

Even if you've layered window treatments to eliminate noise, make sure they can be fully opened to let in as much sunlight as possible during the day. It'll go a long way toward brightening and expanding any space. Overhead light is to be minimized, as it's just too harsh to be pretty. Instead, load up on table and floor lamps.

When it comes to pretty paint colors in urban settings, I tend toward greens and blues. These colors of nature are soothing and improve mental, emotional, and physical well-being. People often gravitate to white for walls in smaller rooms because they think it'll open up the space and make it feel larger, airy, and bright. I can't argue with that, especially because it also makes it easy to introduce color in other ways. But dark walls can have a surprisingly similar effect to white ones, especially at night, when deep hues blur corners, causing the sides of a room to almost disappear.

Wrapping a space in a boldly patterned wallcovering will also visually expand a room. Try vertical stripes, for example, to lift low ceilings. (If patterns aren't your thing, consider grass cloth, suede, or another textured material.) To make beautiful use of prints in a small space, deploy them in various places in different ways: as a wall covering at one scale, on an upholstered chair in another, and then as trim on a pillow.

In the city, the directive to embrace symmetry is perhaps the most important of the Principles of Pretty. Pairs of chairs or table lamps, bookshelves, or stools—whether perfectly matched or simply complementary—help you achieve an overall sense of order, calm, and serenity that the best urban settings share. You'll see just how to work with symmetry, and the other principles and elements here, in the four residences featured in the following pages.

Use dark tones to punctuate an otherwise light and bright room. This works wonders when it comes to adding depth and grounding the space.

ATLANTA AERIE

his perfect little pied-à-terre is where my husband and I stay when we're working on projects in Atlanta or checking in on our store there. Jim and I designed it to be an oasis of pretty in the middle of the city's bustling Buckhead neighborhood. The two-bedroom apartment sits on the sixteenth floor of one of two high-rise towers that were among the first skyscrapers built in Atlanta, back in the late 1960s. The towers are beloved for their light-filled apartments' floor-to-ceiling windows, which offer sweeping views of downtown and Buckhead. We bought a unit that hadn't been touched since it was built, then turned it into the city home of our dreams. Jim handled the layout and interior architecture, adding neoclassical molding and wall paneling, while I took on decorating duties. I had two competing visions: a serene ivory palette, set off by dark wood antiques and black accents, and an apartment encased entirely in chintz. Thanks to a gorgeous new Cowtan & Tout fabric I found, with gray-blue and brown hydrangeas and roses on an ivory background, I was able to have it both ways—and all in a home of just 1,500 square feet. Pale, barely there hues and dark woods define the bedrooms and the living room, off of which is a cozy family room with the floral on the walls, curtains, and a few chairs. The ivory tones act as a beautiful connective theme throughout. Jim and I were both thrilled with the outcome.

In the relatively small foyer of our Atlanta apartment, I wanted plenty of interesting objects to see as you passed through: wall paneling, vintage furniture, polished metals, and an art light in the shape of a shell above two works by Jean-Pierre Bourquin.

I did our living room in complementary shades and textures of ivory, with accents coming from the art, pillows, and rug. The antique wood tables and cabinets are all from different eras, but they look modern because of their clean, simple lines.

Especially in a space as neutral as this one, metallic elements bring a bit of luxury and refinement. The golden hues around the room also add a sense of rhythm and balance to the design. The photograph above the sofa is by Josef Hoflehner.

20

We found this stunning Art Deco buffet at an antique fair in the South of France and immediately knew it would become the statement piece in our living room. We bought the pair of armchairs and the mirror in Paris, turning the whole space into a lovely memento of our French travels.

In a galley kitchen, floating wall shelves provide space and air. The shelves are worth sacrificing some enclosed storage space for because they are perfect for displaying favorite pieces as well as everyday items you want to access easily. The artwork is by Richard Giglio.

I love to wrap an entire room in one pattern—it feels so cozy, warm, and welcoming—and in this den I got to do it with one of my favorite fabrics. I used the same Cowtan & Tout linen floral print on the walls, curtains, and upholstery.

TAKE A PRINT AND RUN WITH IT

The colors and materials for the den were born out of my love for this gray-blue and brown floral—and my desire to go big with chintz. Once I'd found the fabric and picked the leopard-print rug, I knew the other elements—including the peach painting by Shelley Reed—would have to be subtle. A chocolate-colored linen velvet, oatmeal-hued wool, smaller leopard print, and fretwork tape did just the trick, creating a space that's as cozy as it is pretty.

Creating a beautiful sanctuary for sleeping is really about distilling
your design down to just a few elements. Start by stripping out
any unnecessary colors or patterns. Use primarily solids, limit
yourself to just a few hues, then play with low-contrast variations
in tone and plenty of soft but interesting textures.

In smaller, windowless bathrooms, keep your design bright and clean-lined.

You'll want to find the perfect open vanity, then add plenty of large mirrors, polished metallic elements, and sources of dimmable light both overhead and on the walls.

These elements create a spa-like atmosphere even if the raw space doesn't feel so soothing.

Storage will be at a premium in a relatively compact bathroom. We wanted to use an open vanity to create the illusion of more space, so we found room for shelves in the wall opposite. They turned out to be a better, more accessible spot for towels and other accoutrements.

MIX FURNITURE FROM DIFFERENT PERIODS

Furniture from the eighteenth and nineteenth centuries is wonderful, but you can add the patina of age to a room just as beautifully with vintage items made much more recently. Here, pieces that date back to, or are inspired by, the 1940s and 1950s ground these spaces with a sense of the past, but their clean modern lines do so in a way that doesn't feel old or old-fashioned. Instead, they look entirely of the moment.

THE SOFTER SIDE OF MODERN

---

the owner of this four-story townhouse in Atlanta's Buckhead neighborhood has a personal style that's modern but classically tailored and with a soft edge—characteristics that are perfectly primed for pretty. Here, in a maisonette built as part of the city's Waldorf-Astoria hotel, she wanted a neutral palette, sensuously curving lines, rich tactile materials, and shimmering metallic accents. This mix of elements, carried from room to room throughout the residence, made for a serene but seductive city retreat in which the owner's collection of modern art could shine.

The idea of a gentle embrace guided every aspect of the design. In the first floor's joint living and dining room, for example, the pieces of furniture—the contemporary sofa and armchairs and the vintage Silas Seandel brass cocktail tables—seem to be reaching out to each other. They look like they're interacting, which makes the design conversational, alive, and even slightly unpredictable. The combination of the room's richly textured fabrics—such as alpaca, wool, mohair, and leather—keeps the neutral color palette alive and visually interesting. From the first floor to the fourth, the gentle curves of the house's luxe furnishings and the plush surfaces of each of the materials make the interiors feel warm and welcoming. The home's metal accents sparkle like jewelry worn with an ensemble of silk and cashmere.

Curving sculptural elements create an interesting and beckoning seating area in this Atlanta town house, which features a photograph by Andrew Moore. All of the fabrics have a soft and luxurious feel; that tactile element really completes the space.

In a room with both living and dining areas, keep the colors consistent and use the furnishings to define each space. Here, the seating addresses the fireplace while the table and chairs are centered on the window and the opening to the adjacent kitchen.

38

Upholstered dining chairs can help soften a shape that might otherwise feel like it's too modern and spare. They bring comfort and a sense of pretty to the table.

A pewter hood, brass light fixtures, and brushed stainless strapped cabinets prove it's more than just OK to combine metals in a kitchen—it's recommended. As the late, great decorator Charles Faudree used to say, "It's all about the mix, not the match." The artworks above the banquette are by Raymond Debieve.

A mirror-tile mosaic backsplash, a brass counter, and heavy
hand-blown crystal orb pendants help this bar bring on the bling.
OPPOSITE: Banquettes, pedestal dining tables, and armchairs with
interesting silhouettes are a favorite combination of mine—much more
inviting and comfortable than just a standard table and chairs.

FRAME AND HANG ART WITH CARE

The mat and the frames that you choose for your artworks can completely change not only their size but the feeling they bring to a room. Smaller pictures made larger by bigger framing, for example, will appear more important and substantial. When grouping works together on a wall, I select pieces that have

similar palettes and figures or shapes, and then mat and frame them to coordinate. Doing so will give you the prettiest results, as will laying out and measuring a gallery wall on the floor before you hang. It's also a very good idea to hire a professional to do the hanging for you. That's something much harder than it looks!

PRETTY PALETTES

LET GLAMOUR REIGN SUPREME

The silver tones of the master bedroom's seating area were conceived to create a luxe oasis in which to rest, relax, and recharge. Soft, luxurious fabrics led the design, and shimmering elements serve as accents: wallpaper with pearlized studs and wool-and-silk curtains with sparkling trim. Everything is done in a gradient of the same hushed gray hue, echoed in the painting by Brian Coleman.

One of my favorite tricks in a substantial bedroom is to place large mirrors over commodious bedside tables with an oversized lamp in front. Doing so fills the available wall space, opens the room up, and helps move light around. The painting is by Zhao Kailin.

50

When designing workspaces
in residences, always emphasize
"home" over "office."

Look for ways to let in natural light,
use ultra-soft materials and calming
colors, and think about maximizing
comfort everywhere you can.

Select art that brings you absolute
joy, and hide anything that doesn't:
screens, cords, paperwork.

You'll end up with a room as
relaxing as it is inspiring.

As more and more clients request home offices, I have learned that these rooms can be creative. Here, I used a curved desk, furry ottoman, shearling armchair, and funky brass drinks table to turn an office into an unexpected surprise. The painting is once again by Zhao Kailin.

This all-white bathroom, with its mosaic marble floor and large soaking tub, celebrates the natural light that pours in from two huge windows. OPPOSITE: When space is at a premium in a bedroom, use a desk or dressing table to do double duty as one of the nightstands.

CREATE A FOCAL POINT WITH ART

Few design elements capture attention in a room like a single piece of statement art—like these works by, from left, Shawn Dulaney, Lourdes Sanchez, and Paolo Ceribelli. Beautifully framed and matted and then hung over a console table or sideboard, they require very little in the way of accessories. Exact symmetry isn't necessary, but try to balance the accents from one side to the other. This draws the eye toward the art, allowing it to remain the star of the show.

SLEEPING PRETTY

lthough it turned out to be the absolute picture of pretty, the design of this master suite wasn't without its challenges. The room's imposing overall size, with ultra-high ceilings, soaring windows, and expansive square footage, lent it a feeling of cavernousness rather than the coziness you crave from a bedroom. My solution was to divide the space into two parts—a sleeping area and a sitting area—and to use pieces of furniture that, while substantial and dramatic enough to hold their own in the large room, still felt human in scale. The very first thing I did was to commission a large, romantic canopy bed; this helped split both the height of the space and its area in half, creating a room within the room and adding the intimacy that was previously lacking. The bed's substantial canopy and hangings are all done in satin and silk in various shades of pale celadon and ivory, hues that continue into the living area. There, the furniture is similarly large in scale, but it all still feels light thanks to legs that lift nearly every piece—the limestone-topped black-iron coffee table, the Italian desk, and the pairs of large club chairs and more petite French fauteuils—off the sheepskin rug. Above the sofa hangs a six-panel antique coromandel screen whose impressive size and dark color help ground the large, light-colored room, preventing it from feeling like it could just float away. Above the mantel, meanwhile, an oversized Fabiola Jean-Louis portrait of a hauntingly beautiful and strong woman (I call her the modern Mona Lisa) watches over the room, *her* room, with large brown eyes. She's very feminine and very beautiful, but in the most striking of ways—just like this room itself.

I always like to incorporate seating in a bedroom—a chaise longue or a chair and ottoman, even a sofa if there's space. Ultimate relaxation requires the ability to prop your feet up. A figurative monotype by Otto Neumann hangs below an antique watercolor.

In this master suite, a restrained use of color was key. All of the fabrics are different fibers (including wool, linen, silk, and cotton), but they are all exactly the same two colors, which creates a peaceful and pretty setting. The portrait is by Fabiola Jean-Louis.

The antique coromandel screen, originally created as a room divider, hangs over the sofa like a work of art. It serves several purposes, adding a darker tone in an otherwise light room, filling a vast wall, and making the ceiling height seem lower and more human in scale.

Work feels like pleasure when done at a beautiful desk bathed by natural light. OPPOSITE: This grand canopy bed makes a dramatic statement. Although it is generous in size, its color palette keeps it feeling pretty rather than heavy or old-fashioned.

PRETTY PALETTES

BE DISCIPLINED ABOUT COLOR

Sticking to a spare color scheme is one of the simplest of pretty principles. In this bedroom, a particular shade of pale celadon and another of ivory are repeated again and again: in the curtains, in the canopy bed's hangings, and in the upholstery of both the bed itself and the furnishings of the adjacent seating area. When done in limited colors, beautiful materials—like the embroidery, linen, silk, wool, and faux fur here—can be better appreciated.

URBAN OASIS

---

his expansive, four-bedroom house in Atlanta sits in a neighborhood of charming hundred-year-old residences that's one of the city's most hidden gems. Accessed by a side road off a busy street, its tree-planted sidewalks and almost storybook-style architecture seem worlds away from the skyscrapers of downtown—even though the heart of the city is just a short, ten-minute drive from your front door. It's a prized location because you just have no idea how close you are to the city.

The new owners of this 1920s English Tudor house wanted it to serve as a relaxing hideaway, a welcome contrast to their busy, high-powered professional lives. To help take the edge off as soon as they walk through the front door, we worked with a deeply calming palette that played with shades of duck-egg blue, used in both large swathes and subtle accents, but always in low-contrast ways. This palette combines with a certain sense of restraint and delicacy to create the prettiest of spaces. The carefully considered furniture floor plans use pairs of chairs, sofas, tables, and more to create a balanced sense of symmetry. To this, we added a limited number of tightly edited accessories. There's no extra fluff. We wanted the rooms to be clean, uncluttered, and calm, designed for two people who have no room in their lives for more complication. As for the delicacy, it stems largely from the lines of the furniture in each room—the gentle taper of the surprisingly slim posts of the master suite's four-poster bed, for example, and the Maison Baguès–style cocktail table in the living room. The result is a home that's an impressively serene city refuge, even within the quiet of its suburban-style neighborhood.

The living room's little window alcoves were already so storybook-sweet that no window treatments could possibly make them any more appealing. I left them free of curtains and shades.

While I always look for other, more hidden options, sometimes the only place for a television is on the wall over the mantel. Here, the black rectangle of the firebox echoes that of the screen, providing a bit of balance and lessening the TV's visual impact.

ACCENT COLORS MATTER

The prettiest way to set off a neutral palette is with a single additional hue, one that is similarly saturated but also different in tone than the base color. In this living room, a light duck-egg blue—which appears throughout the home—can be seen in the pillows, curtains, trim, and art. It is nearly as pale as the ivory background, but its coolness provides contrast. A large painting by Shawn Dulaney is entirely in keeping with the scheme, as are the smaller works by Michael Abrams.

This small dining room is serene, thanks largely to its floor-to-ceiling palette of duck-egg blue. The door on the left is a closet, while the one on the right leads to the kitchen. We mirrored the previously clear glass on the latter to create symmetry.

74

PRACTICAL CAN BE BEAUTIFUL

A color scheme this light can work anywhere, even in a high-traffic, multipurpose family room. How? Most of the solid textiles on the upholstered pieces are outdoor fabrics, which provide durability even in pale hues. Tape trims and decorative cords create thoughtful dressmaker detailing, while the bare floors, beadboard walls, and painted furniture are forgiving of the inevitable wear and tear. The art by Claudia Thomas complements the space.

I custom designed this slim little bed to suit the room and chose a pale painted finish for it. The piece provides the height the room needs without the heft of a more traditional dark wood four-poster. The work over the fireplace is by Dusty Griffith.

Sometimes less is more when it comes to window treatments, especially when utter privacy and total darkness don't have to be priorities.

Bringing in sunlight, celebrating the reflectivity of glass, and making a room feel like it extends into the outdoors can be much more important goals.

That doesn't mean your windows need to be completely naked, however. I love sheers, café curtains, and unlined woven blinds—which all softly filter light— to get the best of both worlds.

I couldn't be happier about the renewed popularity of café curtains. They're perfect when you want to let in natural light but still give yourself some privacy. I especially love them in bathrooms and kitchens. And, because they require half the fabric, they're half the cost of regular curtains.

PRETTY ROOMS IN THE

country

today, many of us may think of country houses as rustic or rugged, or even barn-like. But some of the prettiest homes I've ever been in anywhere are the elevated estates and manors—aristocratic and otherwise—of bucolic properties in England and France. It's the beautifully styled rooms of these sorts of residences that I keep top of mind when thinking about the Principles of Pretty in the country.

That doesn't mean a rural farmhouse, mountaintop retreat, or wooded cabin has to have a certain formality, or that it has to take inspiration from the eighteenth and nineteenth centuries. Remember, pretty doesn't have to be fancy or old-fashioned—in fact, it usually isn't—and it's the furthest thing from fussy. But you'll find that pretty is most successfully achieved in the country when you add sophisticated and refined elements into the mix. They help smooth out some of the rough edges that so often come with the pleasures of pastoral living.

Within the relatively rugged architectural shell of a converted barn, say, or a wood-beamed chalet, or a log cabin, the principles are particularly capable of creating an atmosphere of warmth, comfort, and ease. Soft, pretty elements serve as the more feminine yin to balance the masculine yang of the architecture.

Just imagine the softness of overstuffed upholstered furniture in a wood-paneled great room, or, in a guest room, a canopy or four-poster spool bed piled high with hand-embroidered pillows and fluffy feather duvets. Picture a dining room centered on a long, inviting farm table surrounded by comfortable upholstered chairs and set with heirloom china, all atop a casual wool plaid or hooked rug. A welcoming, generously sized fireplace becomes the central element of

In a space with soaring height, try to keep the furnishings human in scale instead of reaching for the ceiling: Using low-slung pieces will make the room feel cozier.

A space with symmetrical architecture usually cries out for symmetrical interior design. Pairs bring a sense of calm and order and feel balanced. Here, we even added curtains in the opening between the living room and foyer to echo those in the window. I commissioned the large landscape painting over the mantel from artist Bob Christian.

almost any pretty country home, designed with ample space to gather in front of it, finished with attractive storage for logs, kindling, and tools. Think about a vintage quilt thrown over the back of a club chair in front of that roaring fireplace, or used as a wall hanging or even as material to upholster an accent piece. These are some of the elements that make pretty possible in the country.

Your country palette, meanwhile, will be at its prettiest when it pulls largely from what you see through your windows, taking its cues from nature: the greens of meadow and mountain vistas, the blues of the sky, the tans and taupes of the earth, the grays and browns of boulders and cliffs, the reds and siennas of earth and clay. Mix solids in these hues with such country-appropriate prints as toile and mattress ticking, checks and gingham, plaids and stripes. Chintz and florals have their place, too. Vary the scale of the patterns you deploy in each room, some large, some small, and don't be afraid to have several of them in any one space.

As you select materials, stick to natural fabrics with softness: cotton, linen, and wool; leather and suede; velvet and corduroy. And be sure to use plenty of wood—whether painted, stained, or raw—especially on walls. Incorporate rough-hewn, antique, salvaged, or vintage-looking timber beams, posts, and trusses if they're not already part of the architecture. When it comes to stone, the more local it is, the better. In a country house, I love brick or bluestone floors, especially when they're heated.

As you'll see in the homes in the following pages, the Principles of Pretty help you balance a certain relaxed elegance with the casual ease we all seek from country living

Little vignettes speak volumes. Hand-thrown pottery and a mosaic stone table are juxtaposed with a moody landscape by Poogy Bjerklie and a vase of fresh tulips, echoing the mix of rustic earthiness and refined sophistication that defines the rest of the room.

AT HOME IN THE HAMPTONS

lthough this property is in the Hamptons—the seaside retreat on New York's Long Island—it's located slightly inland, so the owners requested a traditional country house look. As a young family with a love of equestrian pursuits, they wanted to create rooms with deep, classically American roots and a dash of folk-art style. Pretty lends itself perfectly to just this sort of decorating, the kind that's grounded in the past but intended for contemporary living. Here, the lightness of the color palette supports the success of the scheme: The palest of pale blues and greens, occasional pinks and yellows, and plenty of whites, ivories, and other barely-there neutrals keep the polished brown wood furniture, classic lines, and plaids and checks from feeling dark and heavy. Even the bedrooms, wrapped in the most traditional of florals, toiles, and stripes, are the furthest thing from old-fashioned. Monochromatic or otherwise low-contrast versions of these prints heighten the youthful sensibility. The large windows in these sleeping quarters, like those throughout the house, flood the interiors with sun, further emphasizing the freshness. All the curtains can be fully opened, while sheers beneath let in light without sacrificing privacy. I found it incredibly exciting that a couple so young was ready to embrace classical decorating, and I believe that their house is proof positive of the ability of pretty to imbue tradition with a sense of the twenty-first century.

Even on a house up North, a veranda exudes the charm of the South. Here, in New York's Hamptons, we've got all the regional hallmarks of a pretty and proper Southern front porch: wicker, stripes, ferns—and the ultimate sense of welcome.

Low contrast is key to pretty, but it's not the only way. In a beautiful paneled foyer, a dark oak English dresser base and a simple black-painted bamboo bench contrast with the white paneling and grass cloth, even as they blend with the wood floors.

Try stripes on the walls *and* the floor. This carpet is laid so its pattern seems to continue onto the wall. Even the pleats of the curtains seem to follow suit.

94

Round tables, rather than rectangular ones, work best in square or octagonal dining rooms. They simply improve a space's flow and circulation.

With leaves, the circle can expand into an oval for larger parties, so you're not sacrificing space.

They are better for conversation, too, and they're almost always prettier than their rectangular alternatives.

In a dining room without curtains, I like to use fully upholstered chairs. The additional fabric provides an opportunity for more pattern and color, and they're just more comfortable than seats with more exposed hard surfaces. They visually soften the table, as well.

THE BIG BOOK OF HORSES

A vintage birdhouse atop an industrial console makes a strong focal point. OPPOSITE: People love sitting in a booth at a restaurant, so why not build a banquette at home? PREVIOUS PAGES: Wicker and checks are country house essentials, here given a fresh look by a pale, beachy palette.

The same medium-scale check appears on the bed, upholstery, and window treatments in this guest room. Lowering the contrast of the pattern made for a very pretty space; the use of the repeated print soothes and embraces.

PLAY WITH PAINTED FURNITURE

Using various tints of white- or pale-painted wooden furniture in your space
is a great way to add lightness and informality. These finishes read as more
casual than stained wood or darker colors, and they make rooms feel airy
and more spacious—and, therefore, prettier—as a result. It's a trick that's
been deployed in Swedish interiors for centuries. I especially like to use paint
to update antiques, to prevent them from looking frumpy. A coat of paint

can be easier (and more economical) than having furniture stripped and refinished. Keep in mind: The hues you select for painted items in a room should coordinate with each other, but they don't need to match exactly. Usually, it's best if they're slightly different and designed to blend: a pale green with an ivory with a light gray, for example. This gives you some flexibility, especially as you mix them into a scheme with unpainted pieces.

When you want matching patterns for the
curtain fabric and wallpaper in a room,
be sure to compare swatches: Often,
the printing process will cause the same
pattern to appear to be quite different
on different materials. You want to find
one that's a perfectly twinned pair.

106

EMBRACE TRADITIONAL DECORATING

The classics are classics for a reason. Here, I chose a timeless, refined floral for the walls, curtains, and headboard and then pulled the colors for the coordinating fabrics from that most prominent print: a blue wool herringbone, an ivory strie, aqua linens, and a matching tape trim. Painted finishes rounded out this feminine room and kept it light and airy, while the monogrammed bedding seemed right at home.

Bring in whatever garden elements speak to you to create your own vacation spot right at home. Boxwoods, pea gravel, and bistro chairs did the trick here. The result is a stateside garden vignette that could easily be in the South of France.

ON BLACKBERRY FARM

Set amid the rolling foothills of Tennessee's Great Smoky Mountains, the resort that is Blackberry Farm has been inviting people to relax and unwind, tune out and recover, for more than four decades. This is true whether you're a guest of its hotel or you're among the lucky few who've built a vacation house amid its 4,200 acres of pastoral splendor. My longtime clients, professionals with grown children, are in the latter camp, and here they tasked me with creating a beautiful home for them that both celebrated its surroundings and felt primed for hosting weekend house parties. Designed by Drew Kinney and Keith Summerour of Summerour Architects in a way that blends the rustic with the refined, this contemporary cabin cried out for the pretty treatment. The inspiration for all things pretty here began and ended with the various wonderful shades of green foliage all around the property. The homeowners liked the green idea immediately, and I ran with it, using various shades from the views—a rich leafy hue for the master suite here, a deeper moss for a guest room there. Some spaces are entirely wrapped in green, while in others, it becomes more of an accent. The success of the scheme lies in its layers of color and texture and the way that green can seem both casually relaxed and just sophisticated enough.

A rather serious Gothic console and more playful stone botanicals
make a welcoming statement in this uncrowded foyer. The basket below
provides a handy place to hide muddy boots and shoes.

When you introduce a strongly colored fabric into a room—such as the green velvet on the sofa in this living room—temper it with more subtle hues. Here, that meant various neutrals, which complement the stone elements.

114

PRINCIPLES

DIVIDE LARGE SPACES INTO SEVERAL PARTS

An entryway may be large, but you can immediately create a warm and welcoming atmosphere simply by separating a large space into smaller zones. The stone-and-metal center table atop the antique Oushak carpet here defines a sort of room-within-the-room, helping the area against the wall—with the wingback chairs flanking the mirror and the chest of drawers—serve its own purpose as a place to take off boots, check one's reflection, and admire the art and unusual mirror frame made of antique wooden shoe forms.

The lower ceiling and modest size of this kitchen—designed by the house's architects, Keith Summerour and Drew Kinney—make it feel charmingly and comfortably vintage. OPPOSITE: A pale wood table on a black metal base visually connects to the room's washed-wood ceiling and walls and its black iron chandelier and curtain rods. Between the floor-to-ceiling windows, I hung a painting by Clay Wagstaff.

Family rooms can invite you and your guests to spend time together playing games, reading, and relaxing—not just watching TV or practicing video game skills. Create spaces that encourage all these activities, with a games table and chairs, a lounge chair and ottoman, and, always, a big overstuffed sofa. The artwork is by Richard Bowers.

Consider putting the headboard of your bed against a window. You don't get to enjoy the view when you're sleeping anyway, and you can look outside from every other room of the house. The placement works especially well here, giving the bed the feeling of an old-fashioned curtained canopied version—but without any of the potential for claustrophobia.

122

DEPLOY ONE HUE IN A VARIETY OF WAYS

The color scheme for this bedroom proceeds from a pair of primary elements, both celebrating green: the textured grass cloth on the walls and the linen check used for the upholstery and window treatments. The verdant floral on the accent pillows continues the theme, adding some darker tones. This palette is neither feminine nor masculine, making it a great choice for a guest room.

With its warm, enveloping feeling, a saturated wall color can promote restful sleep in a bedroom. Such hues have an aesthetic benefit, too, since art and objects will be set off by the darker color. Keep the space bright with paler furnishings and lighting from both chandeliers and table lamps.

126

REPEAT COLOR AROUND AN ENTIRE RESIDENCE

Weaving a particular hue from one room to the next throughout your entire house can be a cohesive and calming design strategy. In this home, the entire palette is composed of various shades of green, set off by pale neutrals, but this specific mossy color makes an appearance again and again. As a result, it serves as a through line and a welcome and familiar presence wherever and whenever it turns

up, whether it's the paint on the walls, the pattern woven into an accent fabric, or the watercolor of an antique botanical illustration. Because the color was taken from the leafy forest views seen through every one of the house's windows, it also helps merge—and create continuity between—indoors and out, ensuring that the beauty of the natural world can be found within each room.

Plaid isn't just for fabrics and rugs. I love how this tiled floor gives the look of a country plaid, even though it's all marble. OPPOSITE: Keep guest rooms simple, largely avoiding personal objects and mementos. Provide visitors with everything they need and nothing they don't.

PRINCIPLES

BLEND INDOORS AND OUT

When designing rooms like this screened porch, think about how you can encourage them to feel like a bridge from the interior of your home to its surroundings. This rustic, local stone fireplace connects to the pastoral Tennessee geography, while the muted green cushions and teak-framed seating with woven rush backs meld into the wooded background. The room makes a quiet statement rather than a bold gesture.

IN THE CAROLINA MOUNTAINS

Set in the hills of Asheville, North Carolina, a stone's throw from the Vanderbilt family's famed Biltmore Estate, this large house sits under a canopy of beautiful trees. Its grand stone-and-timber construction exudes romance and regional curb appeal, but its interiors needed serious work, requiring a gut renovation. The design direction from the homeowners was simple: "Bring in the pretty," they told me. I couldn't have been happier. We decided that the decorating should serve as a counterpoint to the architecture's more rustic elements—rough-hewn beams, barn-like trusses, local stone fireplaces—to create an air of refinement and polish. Avoiding mountain-decorating clichés, we added dressier fabrics and furniture styles to achieve a feeling of tranquil sophistication throughout. The master suite's iron bed hung with wool hangings is a perfect example of this mixture of rough and smooth, hard and soft, masculine and feminine. In the family room, we started with sheer curtains to soften the perimeter, then layered in neutrally hued wools and linens for the upholstery and rugs. For the living room, we used soft plaid wool curtains to frame the pale-painted wood paneling on the walls, then designed comfortable seating arrangements that both open to the fireplace and encourage conversation. The dining room, for its part, features chairs whose full skirts extend all the way to the floor, a formal note among otherwise more casual furnishings. This house definitely hit my pretty sweet spot, and that of the owners, too.

When you're looking for a piece of furniture to set against a stair railing, try a skirted table. Choosing one softens a space and offers some contrast to the vertical elements of the balustrade.

A series of pendants in a long hallway draws the viewer's attention
down its entire length. OPPOSITE: Let your fireplace be a focal point
by minimizing accents around it. PREVIOUS PAGES: Pulling seating
toward the center of a large space makes conversation easier
and creates easy circulation around the room's perimeter.

With a dressy chandelier, monochromatic palette, and two dozen petite botanicals, this dining room is unabashedly pretty—a wonderfully unexpected surprise given its rustic mountain location.

A custom stove hood becomes a beautiful, dramatic statement. This one completes a space laid out by talented Atlanta kitchen designer Matthew Quinn. I collaborated with him by selecting finishes and fixtures.

PRINCIPLES

WHEN IT COMES TO COFFEE TABLES, BIGGER IS VERY OFTEN BETTER

Large rooms in houses built for families and group entertaining require a *lot* of seating, and *that* requires a lot of space to put down coffee mugs and glasses, to pass around trays with snacks and hors d'oeuvres, and yes, even to put your feet up. An ample coffee table perfectly fills the space–and bridges the gap in the conversation area–that can form in the center of a room whose sofas and chairs are all arranged around the perimeter.

144

In a master suite, the bedrooms and bathrooms should appear related,
something easily achieved by repeating color. Here, the beautiful soft blue-gray
of the sleeping space appears in the bathroom's slipper chair and towels.

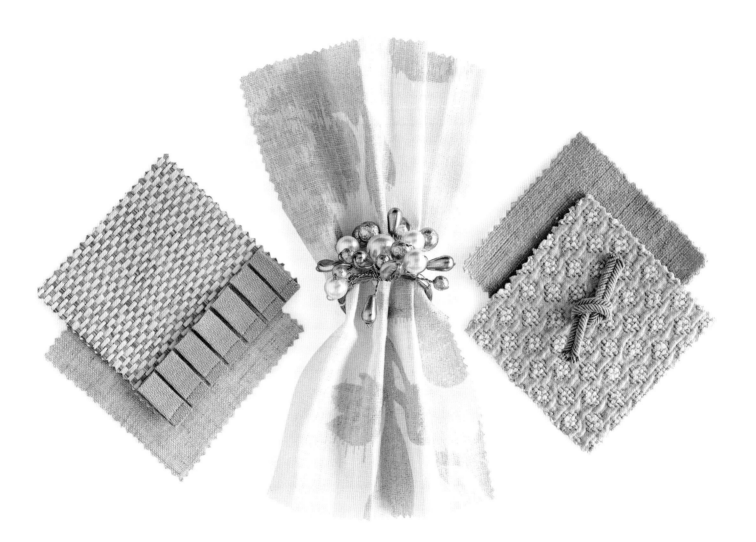

LET COLOR LIGHTEN THE LOAD

If you find yourself concerned that a large piece of dark wood furniture might appear heavy in a smaller space, try adopting a suite of soft, pale hues to make it work. Here, a neutral floral roman shade and embroidered pillows combine with the solid oatmeal-hued rug and other fabrics. As a result, the four-poster bed ends up looking just right.

Use opposing rustic and refined elements to create harmony.

In a space with architectural features inspired by rugged surroundings— rustic trusses, say, or a massive stone mantle—try layering in sheer curtains, lush fabrics, and pale rugs.

These provide the perfect push-pull between hard and soft, masculine and feminine.

When I first visited the house, this space was divided into two: a small room off the kitchen and then a screened porch beyond. I thought that taking down the partition wall and replacing the screens with windows would create a much more usable area: the sort of multipurpose great room that the house needed.

FAMILY MATTERS

---

although this space was created for a house in Atlanta, it has a particularly pastoral atmosphere. That was born out of two facts: the home's location in a leafy, wooded section of the city's Buckhead district, and the Georgian Colonial aesthetic of the house, which was sensitively preserved during a renovation by architect Yong Pak. Part of a new and historically inspired addition, this family room—with its beadboard walls, tray-vaulted beamed ceiling, and large metal windows and doors—called for some country inspiration. I began by painting the walls and ceiling a crisp white and hanging a large lantern-style chandelier that might have looked out of scale anywhere else. Taken together, these design moves cut against the room's rusticity and potential cavernousness, creating something that is more beautiful than it is barn-like. Designing with a young family in mind, we added plenty of comfortable, flexible seating: pairs of sofas, upholstered armchairs, and small wooden bobbin chairs, all arranged around a large, square, skirted storage ottoman. In a corner, a couple of wingback chairs sit at a round table that's perfect for two-person games or more intimate conversations. The étagères flanking the large bi-fold glass-and-steel doors provide space for family photos and memorabilia while also framing the view to the alfresco fireplace in the courtyard beyond. That easy access to the alfresco space allows the room to encourage indoor-outdoor living as much as it calls out for cozy cocooning.

When you have a large room with high ceilings, select a hanging light fixture that can stand up to and balance the scale of the room. Sometimes, to check to see if the size of the pendant, chandelier, or lantern seems right, it is helpful to make a cardboard template of it and hang it in the space.

I always like to vary the height of
furnishings in a room, but never more
so than in a space that's big and tall.
It keeps the room from falling flat.
Here, the étagères balance the scale of
the doors, while the round mirrors above
help draw the eye even further up.

USE PRINT AND PATTERN TO MAKE A LARGE SPACE COZY

In this expansive family room with soaring ceilings and big windows, the goal was to make a slightly cavernous space feel comforting. Pattern proved the way to achieve that: a dynamic and lively embroidered fabric for the curtains, lined with a smaller scale check, strie linen velvet for the sofa, ticking stripes on the ottoman, and a medallion pattern on the club chairs and pillows. The painting by Alexis Portilla appears to have another pattern all its own.

Large storage ottomans are great for holding toys, blankets, or extra pillows in family spaces, and they're soft for putting your feet up, too. Placing a basket on top makes them more usable for holding drinks and snacks. OPPOSITE: Create quiet conversation areas to keep capacious spaces hospitable and welcoming.

LOW COUNTRY STYLE

his house feels like it sits deep in the forest, although it's actually on a coastal island in South Carolina's Port Royal Sound, not far from Beaufort. Its natural, wooded Low Country surroundings very much appealed to the owners, but traditional regional decorating did not. Instead of the dark wood walls and painted floors and relatively heavy, primitive furnishings typical of the area, they wanted their house to be light and lovely, elevated and refined, even as it paid homage to its specific location. In response, I created a scheme that I think of as Low Country gone high style. The dark floors remain, but the walls and stolid redbrick mantels are now lightened and brightened with a very pale palette, largely in green, blue, and neutral hues in each room. Traditional Low Country furnishings can be found here and there—the rush-back bobbin chairs in the living room, the plaid rugs elsewhere—but always in unexpected ways, in pastel colors, say, or covered in patterns made up of such neutral tones they're barely noticeable. More rustic elements got layered in as smaller touches: the country crockery and woven baskets set in bookshelves, the horn accessories on the bar, the wrought-iron pendant lamps hanging in several areas, and the dining room's hide rug. Throughout, there's an air of refinement, polish, and femininity.

Find the right furniture proportions for your hallway. These spare, open consoles fill the narrow space without crowding, and their depth offers room for lamps and accessories.

An antique cabinet works as both storage space and unexpected bar. OPPOSITE: A uniquely shaped room requires multiple seating areas, achieved here with a corner banquette complementing a sofa and rush chairs. The art over the mantel is by Clay Wagstaff.

The secret to solving the riddle of additional seating is often found in unusual, one-of-a-kind antique pieces.

If small in stature, these chairs can be moved around to where they are most needed. With their unique silhouettes, they serve as sculptural elements when they're not being used.

Such seats are just the sort of surprise element that will give your room personality and keep the design fresh.

If you see a quirky or odd chair that you like, buy it. You'll always find a spot to work it in, and these little chairs can add personality and interest to a space. I loved this chair so much, it was hard to part with it from my own collection, but I knew what it would add to this space, so I let it go.

Less is very often more. Consider removing upper cabinets from a pass-through to create a more open, light-filled space. OPPOSITE: Because it's painted a pale hue, the chandelier seems to float above the table in this monochromatic, neutral breakfast nook.

When space is tight, leaving no room for nightstands, use swing-arm wall lamps for reading lights.
OPPOSITE: You'd never know it, but we retrofit this antique French commode to hide a TV. With the touch of a button, the screen rises out of the front portion of the top, leaving room for accessories behind.

Nothing new can replace the patina of the old. Current prices on wooden antiques are often less than reproductions. OPPOSITE: A country bedroom needn't overflow with pastoral design elements to feel like a rustic retreat. Just a few simple nods—checks on the window, burlap on the bedside dresser—do the trick.

Screened porches are hallmarks of great country houses. Decorate them with comfort in mind and select a palette, materials, and furniture that connect the indoors with the outside.

PRETTY ROOMS AT THE

beach

interiors by the beach need to accomplish a neat trick: They have to hold their own against the natural beauty all around them, without distracting from it. The Principles of Pretty can help you design spaces that will achieve that very trick, giving you the tools you need to create spaces that complement their surroundings.

Of paramount importance here is the idea of softening color contrasts. Bring in colors from outside your windows, selecting hues that represent a subtle gradient that doesn't jump from light to dark, or from pastel to super-saturated, too quickly. Instead, it should slowly move through a small slice of the spectrum. Imagine the way the blue of the sea darkens from the coast to the horizon, or the way the sand on a beach lightens as it goes from wet to dry. To these, I often add hints of coral, citrus hues, and other tropical accents, depending on the location. Used sparingly, these provide a bit of contrast that works wonders.

Pretty at the beach calls for a lighter look than what you might do in the countryside, or even the city, but that doesn't mean layering is out of the question. In fact, it's still very important. But it requires you to work with relatively lightweight materials—things that have less heft literally, but also visually and texturally. I love to use wicker and rattan, especially with a slightly more open weave that feels particularly airy. Straw and sisal rugs strike the right note on the coast, too, and not just aesthetically. They can take a beating from wet sandy feet, and, when they do wear out, they're inexpensive to replace. Or just keep the floors—in pale wood, coral or shell stones, and terrazzo—blissfully bare.

Raffia and grass cloth add beauty to walls and even tables, and provide just enough texture. Pieces of actual driftwood make perfect sculptural

This loggia proves that blue and white always feel right in a beach house. The palette makes it easy to mix Moroccan tile with casual stripes plus Delft pottery and Chinese porcelain. Nothing matches, but it all mixes.

centerpieces or accents on shelves, while driftwood-finished floors, mill-work, and furniture, both antique and contemporary, keep the look fresh. (There is a place for darker stains by the beach, too—especially vintage West Indies–style pieces in mahogany and ebony.)

Waterfront houses are usually sunshine filled, as well they should be. Natural light is a huge part of what makes them so beautiful, but it's necessary to temper and soften that light, to make sure the overall effect is pretty and not harsh. My go-tos for window treatments are gauzy all-natural fabrics like linen, muslin, and cotton, which suggest Bahamian breezes even on a perfectly still day; try them over room-darkening tortoiseshell blinds.

To all this, layer in whimsical accents that speak of the sea: fan coral placed in bookcases, shells not just displayed in glass bowls but used like mosaic tiles on a vanity or as a mirror frame. They can become like works of art on your walls. There's nothing prettier than pieces formed by nature, and I always prefer the real thing to a ceramic version.

At the beach, my favorite patterns for fabric and wallpaper are stripes, Indian block prints, paisleys, tropical florals, and palm frond prints. (I also love patterned tile in houses near the water.) They all feel pretty but also casual in a perfectly coastal way. I set these off with rich blues and, even more important, large expanses of white—especially white-painted wood walls, which always look crisp and clean.

The rooms and residences revealed in the following pages embrace the colors of the sea and sky and subtly incorporate the natural wonders that are found only on the coast. They demonstrate how you, too, can easily create the simple, serene pleasures of pretty in your own beach house.

When layering natural textures—like the painted wicker chairs, shell chandelier, and driftwood-finished tabletop set against the rough-hewn beams and floor here—you're looking for balance. The relative smoothness of the walls and ceiling, plus the sleeker ceramics, mirror, and glass elements, help achieve that goal.

PALM BEACH STYLE

t he owners of this newly built home in Palm Beach wanted to create a nostalgic atmosphere that would have all the inviting charm and romance of a cottage on an Old Florida property. A focus on pretty nicely suited this idea. The house itself is the result of architect Roger Patton Janssen's scheme, executed by contractor Meghan Taylor of Seabreeze Building, and its style remains true to the area's local vernacular. The exterior's signature curves and regional materials continue in the design of the interiors, where pecky cypress, driftwood, and pale oak keep company with local stone and marble salvaged from churches. I pulled the palette largely from the blues and whites of the ocean and sky and then expanded it to embrace hints of additional color that borrow from tropical flowers and citrus, especially pinky-orange corals and lime greens. These warm tonal accents keep the design energetic. The homeowners also wanted to balance their important collection of modern art with a sense of informality. To make that happen, I juxtaposed the fine art with more soft upholstery and playful patterns—the dining room's woodblock paisley, a powder room's palm print, the living room's two different stripes. The resulting design encourages casual beachfront living, and at the same time, it presents an aura of refinement and thoughtful design. It gives its occupants all the beauty of Palm Beach without any of the stuffy grandeur the area can have. It's Palm Beach at its prettiest—and with a lovely light hand.

The façade of this newly built, traditionally inspired Florida beach house is all about gentle curves, which make visitors feel like they're being welcomed by an inviting embrace. That idea very much carried through into the interiors.

If you want a small space to have big impact, make every element count. In this foyer, the lighting and furnishing are equally strong in their simplicity—an almost monastic idea that has particular rationale here, since the marble floors were reclaimed from a centuries-old church.

The architecture of this living
room—with its arched transom
windows and rather traditional
millwork—felt fairly formal.
To make it right for a relaxed
beach house, I wanted to loosen
up the look of the furnishings.
Stripes, block prints, and an
abaca rug did just the trick.
The artwork, *Untitled (#19)*, 2011,
is by Richard Serra.

HAVE FUN MIXING STRIPES

I love combining stripes of different scales in similar colorways, but I'll admit I was a little apprehensive about covering all of the upholstery in this room with just two different striped fabrics. The homeowner convinced me to give it a try, however, and the space became one of my favorite rooms in the house. It works so well because the hand-blocked Indian patterns on the curtains and throw pillows provide a counterpoint.

186

NOMAD DELUXE

DONALD JUDD
PRINTS AND WORKS IN EDITIONS

DAVID HOCKNEY

Edited by
Chris Stephens
Andrew Wilson

SCHELMANN

RICHARD SERRA DRAWING

ROBERT MANGOLD

ANDY GOLDSWORTHY

After years of practice, I've
developed a foolproof formula for
arranging items on a coffee table.

Start with something tall slightly
off center. Then layer on low
stacks of books with an item or two
on top, for added interest.

Be sure to have something living
or otherwise fresh—a plant,
fruit, flowers—and always pull
in the colors of the room.

The spines and covers of coffee table books can offer great—and just enough—color contrast in a room with a monochromatic or otherwise fairly simple palette. The splashes of orange on these volumes echo the clementines in the low porcelain bowl and complement the overall blue-and-white scheme.

In a dining room with fairly busy wallpaper, I left most of the room white or, in the case of the table, neutral natural wood. The items on the table echo the woodblock print of the walls.

MAKE A STATEMENT WITH YOUR WALLS

You have my permission—actually, my unadulterated encouragement—to be bold on your walls. It's a great way to liven up a space and give it some place-defining personality. I like powerful patterns, whether in the form of ceramic tiles, wallpapers, or hand-painted murals. They can run the gamut from abstract prints to those that are more organic and naturalistic. My

advice is to choose something fun and a little unexpected and then feel free to add the element of surprise, as long as that surprising element connects (in one way or another) to the style or setting of the house. And remember: Statement walls don't mean you have to decorate the rest of a room quietly. Sometimes, they can turn the volume up for the entire space.

Want to have more fun at home? Install a working bar in a central spot, then enjoy it for drinks or even casual dinners. Nothing feels as festive and lively. Here, the pewter-topped, two-tier counter with drink well and the dark walls make the atmosphere particularly authentic. The painting, *What Summer*, 2012, is by Donald Baechler.

ABOVE AND OPPOSITE: The most comfortable and beautiful alfresco living areas evoke the feeling of an interior space. PREVIOUS PAGES: A favorite of Elsie de Wolfe's at the start of the last century, lattice rooms subsequently fell out of favor, but nothing—nothing!—brings a garden feeling inside like one. Over the sofa hangs a photograph by Michael Gaillard Studio.

It may seem obvious, but it bears repeating: There just isn't anything that goes better with organic elements, motifs, and materials than the color green. Add some white into the mix for crispness, and you've got a winning scheme. My friend Bunny Williams designed the white plaster garden panel hanging over the sofa.

An all-white envelope allows
you to introduce an accent color
in both bold and subtle doses.
A tropical-feeling coral hue
appears throughout this room,
but in very different ways, from
pale to super-saturated, and in
a variety of patterns.

Dream Catcher   Margaret A. Salinger

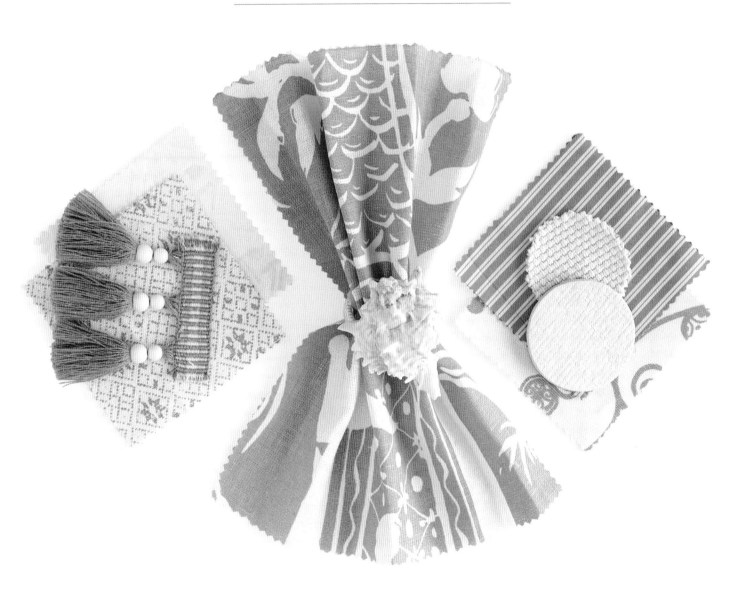

USE FRESH COLOR TO UPDATE TRADITION

Linen curtains in a chinoiserie pattern prove that even the most classic of motifs can be made current. The secret here is the use of a cheerful coral color. I let this fabric take center stage, adding matelasse, ticking stripes, fun trims, and a select few other patterns in supporting roles.

Laying some colorful groundwork—in this case, the coral-hued carpet—lends a space a playful feeling that's just right in a beach house guest room. Also perfect for these sorts of spaces: Extra-long twin beds, which can be pushed together to create a king-size spot to sleep. The painting is by Claudia Thomas.

A flamingo wallpaper gives this bathroom a certain wit and whimsy, but the print's minimal contrast and neutral palette keep it from being too cute. OPPOSITE: Stools at the foot of a bed work well to provide seating in a tight space without room for chairs.

DISCOVER THE FUN OF DECORATING WITH STRIPES

I love stripes everywhere, especially in beach houses. They're casual and fun, and they come in so many different forms, they never feel like they're repeating themselves. There's not a surface that you can't use stripes for, nor a material that you can't find in a striped pattern. Striped ceramic tiles in a pool house bathroom serve to make a small space seem wider, and a striped bed skirt, headboard, and curtains beautifully echo a beadboard ceiling in a bedroom. In a breakfast nook—featuring *Wood Pot with Plant #3*, 2015, by Jonas Wood—the wide awning stripes blend with narrower gauge lines.

WATERFRONT RETREAT

a house that sits directly on the water requires special handling. You need to make sure that the interiors can hold their own against a spectacular view. The owners of this particular home—a charming shingle-style residence—wanted the decoration to take direct inspiration from its beachy surroundings and its vistas of water and sky, including gorgeous sunsets. To bring the house up to its full potential, we realized it needed a major renovation. I enlisted my husband, Jim, to help me add in much-needed architectural details and to rearrange the rooms to take better advantage of the waterfront setting. Once we determined what the new spaces and embellishments would be, my team and I set about gathering fabrics, rugs, and wallpapers to imbue the house with a sense of air, water, and light. The goal was to create a peaceful, restful sanctuary that would encourage the owners and their guests to relax and recharge every time they entered the house. Everything needed to be comfortable and inviting, and nothing was to feel off limits or formal. Pulling from a palette of light blues, pale greens, and various ivories, we worked with natural materials, including linens, cottons, wools, and sheers. We then designed layers of window treatments that would frame and enhance the views. The result is a home that reflects the beauty of its surroundings to create the prettiest of interiors.

Sometimes decorating is about knowing when to do nothing—or almost nothing. This gracefully curving staircase with Chippendale-style balustrade is so beautiful, the foyer required very little else to make it sing.

Because the walnut Steinway piano in this living room is such a showpiece, I wanted all the other wood furnishings in the space to echo it in tone. Rich walnuts and mahoganies add depth and dimension to an otherwise light and neutral palette.

215

The living area's pair of tall arched mirrors serve both to reflect light around this lovely space and to frame its opening to the adjacent dining room—highlighting the enticing peek offered from one room to the next.

216

Many homeowners these days think they don't need a dining room, but when space allows, I always suggest planning for one. Nothing can replace the experience of sharing meals in a beautiful space that's specifically designed for that purpose.

218

A round breakfast table nestles perfectly into the kitchen's bay of windows. OPPOSITE: Most stone slabs are around ten feet in length, so it's best to keep your kitchen island no longer than that, or your countertop will require a seam.

PRINCIPLES

EMBRACE YOUR SOFTER SIDE

A pale palette isn't necessarily a feminine one. Light blues and greens turn this family room into a peaceful and tranquil sanctuary where everyone can gather and be comfortable together. The colors and tones take their cues from the water views beyond the many windows. They're soft and pretty, to be sure, tending toward the feminine, but clean-lined furnishings with almost no embellishments keep everything in balance.

223

The prettiest bookcases leave nothing to chance. Plan their contents as carefully as the rest of the room.

Doing so is simple: Choose at least three anchor items and distribute them among the shelves in a balanced but not totally symmetrical way. Start by placing the largest piece first, then fill in by beginning at the top shelf and working your way down.

Always remember to stand back and check your work often.

These built-in bookshelves—which surround a limestone fireplace with herringbone firebricks in a family room—house a rhythmically displayed collection of celadon ceramics, favorite books, and small, framed watercolor landscapes. The white frame around the television helps it disappear against the wall.

The home's polished but playful bar opens to a cozy sitting area. I designed the two spaces to work in harmony: Similar colors tie them together, as do repeated materials, and the bar's mirror-tile backsplash literally reflects the seating area.

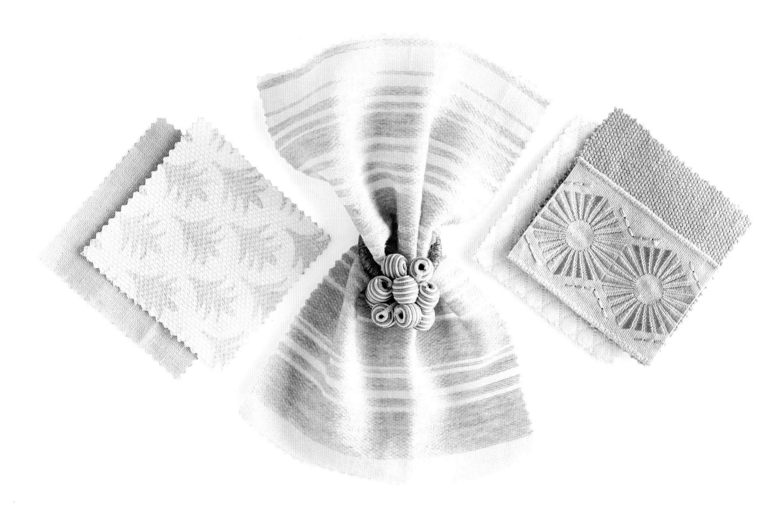

TRY LIMITING YOURSELF TO TWO COLORS

A soft sky blue and simple, clean ivory were all the color needed to make the canopy bed area of this guest room both indulgent and welcoming. Wool striped sheers mixed with matelasse, linen, and beautiful passementerie furnish the space with softness, calm, and the promise of a wonderful night's sleep. The blues, including those in the coordinating pillows, all match exactly, while the silver mirror over the bed amplifies the hue.

In a bedroom, I make room for as much comfortable seating as square footage allows. Think about what these sofas and chairs are for and how you might use them. They can, and should, be multifunctional, conducive to resting, reading, and even working, as well as sharing bedtime stories with kids or a drink with your spouse. This seating area is distinct from the blue-upholstered sleeping space thanks to its nearly all-white furnishings.

CREATE MOSAIC TILE FLOORS

In a bathroom, a stone floor can create as much of a statement as a beautiful carpet would in a living room. There are so many materials and colors of tile to choose from that you can find anything you might want. Here, I selected light blue celeste, darker blue Macauba, and white Thassos marble tiles. The finish of the blues is honed, the white polished, giving the floor its particular shimmer.

The tapered posts of this custom bed draw attention to the John Soane-style ceiling of the master bedroom. The bed's spare, chaste, and almost impossibly thin lines make it feel like it's reaching for the sky.

MIX IN ANTIQUE BROWN WOOD FURNITURE

Gleaming mahogany furnishings create the perfect foil for a soft
and pretty pastel color palette. Their warm, dark hues and high
polish make cool, light tones all the more beautiful. I always find a
way to combine old with new: placing an authentic antique in a room
with a convincing, well-crafted reproduction or a contemporary
reinterpretation. Doing so gives the room a sense of history and soul.

236

When designing a master bathroom, think about your favorite hotel or spa. What made it feel special and sumptuous? This bathroom—with its large soaking tub, expansive shower, double vanity, and dressing table—ticks all the luxe boxes.

AIRY ATLANTIC

When it came to this house, in the quirky northern Florida town of Atlantic Beach, pretty meant letting the sweeping ocean views take precedence. Because of that, and the homeowners' desire for a contemporary look with clean lines and lots of white, the design scheme for the house shows pretty off at its most restrained. The building itself is an old 1920s cedar-shake house, with its original creaky floors and wood walls. To transform it into a modern beach house, I used the Principles of Pretty to create a simple, tailored, entirely unfussy design. The palette brings the outdoors in, juxtaposing pale seafoam blues with white, ivory, and sand hues. (All the once-dark, exposed wood got a new coat of white paint.) I wanted the whole place to feel like there was a cool, gentle breeze blowing through. While pattern and texture can sometimes be pretty's best friend, here we needed no such layering. Instead, solids and monochromatic prints rule the roost, creating an atmosphere of calm. True symmetry, not just a sense of balance, enhances this sensibility, providing order and always highlighting the views. So peaceful, soft, and uncluttered is this home that all who enter instantly feel relaxed and at ease.

I discovered this artwork (and artist Brian Coleman) on Instagram. I knew the piece would beautifully echo the form of the mid-century-inspired console and the items atop it.
FOLLOWING PAGES: When creating symmetry with lots of paired items, simple shapes work best. The paintings on either side of the fireplace are by Claudia Thomas.

PRETTY PALETTES

TAKE YOUR COLOR SCHEME FROM DAY TO NIGHT

When the sun is out, this room is all about the view, so its palette both frames and expands
that vista. Soft, watery shades of blue—used for the upholstery, pillows, and, especially,
the curtains—do just that. The room holds its own at night, too, once the view disappears.
The fabrics and colors are just as pretty after dark, when the room itself becomes the view.

Rope-wrapped stools punctuate an otherwise clean, all-white kitchen. PREVIOUS PAGES: The dining area is imbued with a sense of space, air, and light—an echo of its former life as a porch, before it was connected to the living room.

Thanks to the ever-increasing variety of stain-resistant performance fabrics—as well as waterproof outdoor materials that look great inside—family rooms no longer have to be wrapped in dark colors to be kid-friendly. All the textiles here were designed for alfresco use, and the rug is polypropylene, but you'd never know it.

The master bedroom's unusual shape and its walls of windows permitted us to create two distinct seating areas. The pure white scheme ensures that nothing detracts from the water views.

SEA ISLAND STYLE

Pretty took on a starring role in this family home and smoothed over some of the more rustic elements of the decades-old Low Country house, which perches on the edge of the marshes of Sea Island, Georgia. A subtle monochromatic color palette, a variety of soft textures and textiles, and plenty of upholstered pieces ease the ruggedness of the existing timber-framed doorways, rough-hewn floors, and pitched wood ceilings.

Here, the homeowners requested an entirely neutral scheme. That's something completely in keeping with the pretty principle to lower color contrasts, but it could easily fall flat. With the wonderful blue and green views of the surrounding marshes, that was unlikely to happen at this home, but I took no chances. To ensure visual interest, I pulled in plenty of textures, letting the differences between them stand in for color variation. The mix of highly tactile materials—sea grass, wicker, rattan, shells, coral stone, woven rugs, and textiles including linen, cotton, and gauze—is highlighted by smooth accents of glass, polished stone, and wrought iron whose darker hues are set off by the otherwise pale neutrals. The patina of largely eighteenth- and nineteenth-century bleached or whitewashed antiques adds another layer to complete the look.

This Sea Island, Georgia, home enjoys expansive and extremely peaceful views of the Intracoastal Waterway. FOLLOWING PAGES: When designing a series of spaces that are largely open to each other, keep the palette of colors, textures, and materials consistent. That ensures an easy aesthetic flow from room to room, which creates a sense of calm and consistency.

In a room with multiple seating areas, I like to ground each with its own rug. Using separate but matching carpets defines the different spaces while simultaneously connecting them visually. (TV cabinets may feel like a thing of the past, but they shouldn't. This antique Swedish armoire conceals an 85-inch flatscreen!)

PRINCIPLES

LET THE OUTSIDE IN

When a room opens to views as tremendous as this one does, it's always a good idea to incorporate natural elements that echo the surrounding landscape. Here, I knew we had to use an array of highly textured, organic materials and objects that would feel beautifully connected to the marshes of the Intracoastal Waterway just beyond the windows. That meant deploying bleached-wood and wicker seating, stacked oyster-shell lamps and nautilus accents, a jute rug, and a limestone table—all of it designed to ensure that indoors and out would flow together.

If you inherit antique architectural elements, use them as a muse for your design.

Rough-hewn posts and beams, for example, can inspire the use of new textiles and furniture made of such highly textured materials as nubby linen, rattan, and rope.

That allows all the pieces to play nicely together, guaranteeing that everything, both old and new, looks entirely at home.

When decorating a beach house, try to find a comfortable bar stool without fabric on the seat. These cane-and-wicker bistro-style stools are incredibly low maintenance in a kitchen frequented by folks in wet bathing suits.

In bedrooms, high ceilings almost always call out for tall beds, which create cozier, more intimate sleeping spots. The deep footboard of this custom bed hides a television, which rises at the touch of a button and swivels so it can be seen from either side of the room.

ORGANIC AND NATURAL CAN STILL BE REFINED

The materials and colors in this serene master suite sitting area take their cues
from the house's coastal, marsh setting, but in a way that barely brushes
against the rustic. The pale earth tones of the textured grass cloth on the walls,
the wide linen stripe on the sofa, and the wool rug underneath—as well as
the peek through to the bedroom—are relaxed and unfussy yet sophisticated.

When working with matching wallpaper and a fabric-covered headboard,
hang the paper first, then show your upholsterers a picture so they can
make sure the patterns align. OPPOSITE: Painted wooden beds are especially
desirable for a beach house with lots of visitors; nothing is easier to maintain.

ACKNOWLEDGMENTS

t his is my fourth book in eight years. When I look over all of their many pages, one word—besides "pretty"—comes to mind: productive. I am often asked how I manage to do so much: run and buy items for our various stores, spend time with my family, and, of course, decorate the fabulous homes of our fantastic clients around the world, all of which requires nearly nonstop travel. The answer is simple. It's only possible because of my wonderful, creative, and fun staff.

In each of our locations, I have a group of hardworking, dedicated, and talented people who are responsible for the houses that fill this book. Not only do they manage multiple decorating projects at once, they do it in the front of busy home-furnishings stores. Regardless of how involved they are in a design project, when people walk in, those customers are greeted with a smile and treated like the important clients they are. The staff in my stores are multitasking to an extreme every day, and yet they somehow manage to laugh and have fun together, even when faced with impossible deadlines.

So, to them I want to say that I don't even know where to begin, because "thank you" seems inadequate. I see how hard you work and how devoted you are, not only to me, but also to our craft. I think we are building something significant and important together, and I couldn't have written this book, or any other, without you. You make my life a joy and work seem like fun. I am grateful for every contribution you make and every minute that you spend running the stores and managing our clients.

The photographers and stylists who created the images here ensure that all the rooms you see look their very best. That's also true of the talented architects and diligent contractors who made these houses possible, not least of all my husband, Jim, who collaborated with me on many of these projects. (Our greatest collaborations, however, are our children, two of whom work with us and all of whom have become my support network in everything that I do.)

Book designer Doug Turshen and his colleague Steve Turner took all the photographers' pictures and turned them into the beautiful object you hold in your hands now. I'd be nowhere without them. Writer Andrew Sessa, meanwhile, teased out of me the details of my passion for pretty, as well as the stories behind each house and the reasons behind every design decision I made, to craft the words filling these pages.

All of my books have found a home at the publishing house Abrams, and I am eternally grateful to Shawna Mullen and her stellar team—managing editor Glenn Ramirez, design manager Danny Maloney, creative director Deb Wood, and production manager Katie Gaffney—for believing in me and my work and then shepherding these volumes from the kernel of an idea to something that readers can page through as a source of design inspiration.

I look forward to working with all of you again, and very soon.

PHOTOGRAPHY CREDITS

J. Savage Gibson Photography
4, 7, 82, 113, 114, 115, 116, 117, 118, 119, 120, 121, 122, 123, 124, 126, 126, 128, 129, 130, 131, 132, 133, 135, 136, 136, 138, 139, 120, 141, 142, 143, 144, 145, 146, 147, 148, 151, 160, 162, 163, 164, 166, 167, 168, 169, 170, 171, 172, 173, 174, 176, 179, 181, 182, 183, 184, 185, 187, 188, 190, 191, 192, 193, 194, 195, 196, 197, 198, 199, 200, 201, 202, 203 204, 206, 207, 208, 209, 210, 211, 241, 242, 243, 244, 246, 247, 248, 249, 250, 251, 252, 253, 255, 256, 257, 258, 259, 260, 261, 263, 264, 265, 267, 268, 269, 271

Max Kim Bee
1, 2, 10, 12, 16, 18, 19, 20, 21, 22, 23, 24, 25, 26, 27, 29, 30, 31, 33, 34, 35, 37, 38, 39, 40, 41, 42, 43, 44, 45, 46, 47, 49, 50, 51, 53, 54, 55, 56, 57, 91, 92, 93, 94, 95, 97, 98, 99, 100, 101, 102, 103, 104, 105, 106, 107, 109, 110, 111, 213, 214, 215, 216, 217, 218, 219, 220, 221, 222, 223, 225, 226, 227, 229, 230, 231, 232, 233, 234, 235, 236, 237, 238, 239

Daniel Barley
28, 48, 66, 76, 108, 125, 149, 157, 186, 205, 228, 245, 266

Emily Followill
68, 70, 71, 72, 73, 74, 75, 77, 78, 79, 81, 85, 86, 87, 89, 153, 154, 155, 156, 158, 159

Robert Peterson for Rustic White Photography
15, 58, 60, 61, 62, 63, 64, 65, 67

Endpaper and title page fabrics courtesy of Cowtan & Tout.
Interiors on pages 52–67, 84–89, and 152–159 created as part of the
Southeastern Showhouse organized by *Atlanta Homes and Lifestyles.*

Editor: Shawna Mullen
Designer: Doug Turshen with Steve Turner
Production Manager: Rachael Marks

Library of Congress Control Number: 2020944171

ISBN: 978-1-4197-4385-6
eISBN: 978-1-64700-292-3

Text copyright © 2021 Phoebe Howard

Cover © 2021 Abrams

Printed and bound in China
10 9 8 7 6 5 4 3

Abrams books are available at special
discounts when purchased in quantity for
premiums and promotions as well as
fundraising or educational use. Special
editions can also be created to specification.
For details, contact specialsales@abrams-
books.com or the address below.

Abrams® is a registered trademark of
Harry N. Abrams, Inc.

ABRAMS The Art of Books
195 Broadway, New York, NY 10007
abramsbooks.com

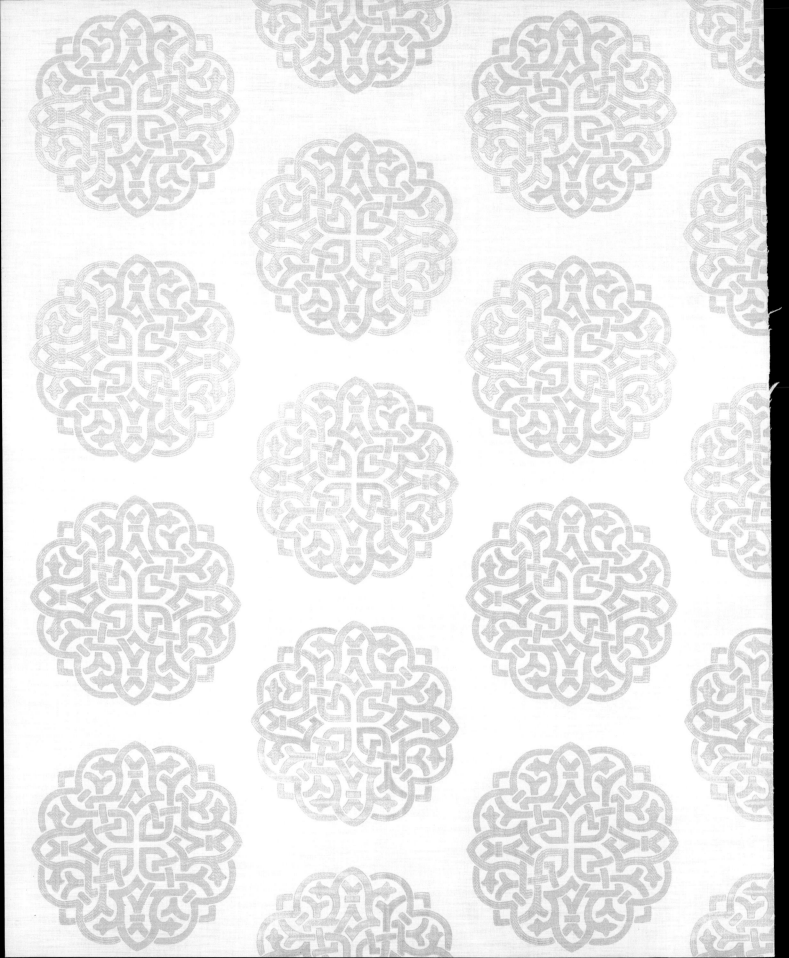